W9-BJK-255

! BEWARE
WE ARE POISONOUS!

HOW ANIMALS DEFEND THEMSELVES

BY
HANS D. DOSSENBACH

BLACKBIRCH PRESS, INC.

WOODBRIDGE, CONNECTICUT

Published by Blackbirch Press, Inc.
260 Amity Road
Woodbridge, CT 06525

Email: staff@blackbirch.com
Web site: www.blackbirch.com

Printed in Hong Kong

10 9 8 7 6 5 4 3 2 1

First published in German as *Achtung, ich bin giftig!*
© 1991 by Kinderbuchverlag Luzern AG

**Library of Congress
Cataloging-in-Publication Data**

Dossenbach, Hans D., 1936–.
    [Achtung ich bin giftig! English]
    Beware! we are poisonous: how animals defend themselves / by Hans D. Dossenbach. — 1st ed.
        p.   cm.
    Includes bibliographical references (p. 39) and index.
    Summary: Examines the characteristics and habits of different kinds of snakes, fish, spiders, insects, and other animals that use poison to defend themselves.
    ISBN 1-56711-215-3 (lib. bdg. : alk. paper)
    1. Poisonous animals—Juvenile literature. I. Title.
QL100.D6513   1999
591.6'5—dc21   97-45490
                                    CIP
                                    AC

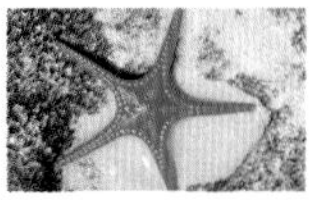

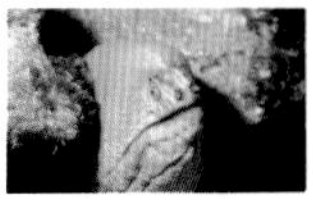

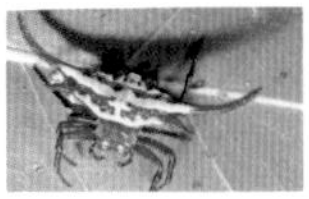

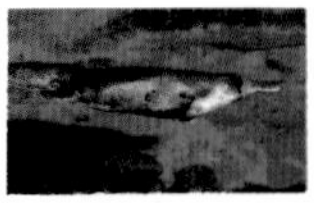

CONTENTS

WEAPONS FOR SURVIVAL

◆ ◆ ◆ ◆ ◆ ◆ ◆

Animals need weapons to survive in the natural world. They need to defend themselves against enemies and to overpower prey. Almost every living thing has some means of protection or defense. Some have sharp teeth, others have pointy beaks. Still others have dangerous claws, talons, horns, or hard hooves.

Some animals have developed weapons of a very special and dangerous kind. These creatures use powerful poisons as their defense. In a way, poisonous animals have a kind of "chemical laboratory" in their bodies. The "laboratory" is a gland or group of glands in which poisonous substances are made.

There is a huge variety of poisonous animals in the natural world. In this book, you'll meet only a small fraction of them. Of all the poisonous creatures, some are more dangerous to humans than others. Certain snakes, scorpions, frogs, and jellyfish are just a few.

Most poisonous animals use their poison not as a weapon of attack, but rather as a defense. And many of these animals have flashy colors that warn others of their dangerous poison. Predators, in turn, recognize these colors as signals of danger. Most of the time they will wisely steer clear of the poisoners.

Perhaps poisonous animals are so fascinating to us because they are dangerous. But many of us think of dangerous animals as "cruel" or "mean." This just isn't true. The truth is that these animals are simply using what nature gave them to survive. In this way, poisonous animals are no different from you or any other living thing.

SNAKES

◆ ◆ ◆ ◆ ◆

Only one in six snakes is poisonous. A few of these are found in North America, but they don't often come in contact with humans. When they do, however, they deserve respect.

Perhaps no other poisonous animals are as feared as snakes. But how dangerous are they, really? It is important to remember that snakes are not "vicious." They are hunters, and their poisonous weapons are primarily for killing their prey. They are not at all interested in killing humans if they feel directly threatened. Ordinarily, they will flee if at all possible.

One reason that snakes sometimes attack is that they are easily surprised. Snakes cannot actually hear, they are completely deaf! And they don't see especially well either. They do, however,

humans—mostly because they can't swallow humans! The largest poisonous snake in the world is the king cobra of India. This snake can grow to 18 feet (6 meters) long, but can only eat a large lizard at most. That's why snakes will only attack

A common viper usually has a dark zigzag band on a gray or brownish background (above left). It is also sometimes solid black (above).
Opposite page, top: Sand vipers can be found in northern Italy, Austria, and as far east as Asia.
Opposite page, below: The European asp viper is widely found in Italy, France, Switzerland, and parts of Germany.

have an excellent sense of smell, which they use to find and follow prey. But they can only recognize the smell of a person if the person is already very close—so close that the snake feels threatened. Snakes are, however, very sensitive to vibrations in the ground. When a human comes near, the snake usually senses these vibrations soon enough to hide before it is seen.

Sometimes, snakes don't pay attention to ground vibrations and stay where they are. During mating times, for example,

are nonpoisonous. The 400 or so species of poisonous snakes can be divided into three major groups: rear-fanged snakes, elapids, and vipers. Rear-fanged snakes have very small poisonous fangs that sit far back in the jaw, where they usually can't do much damage to a human. Nevertheless, there are at least three such tropical species that are known to have killed people. Elapids are mainly found in southern Asia, in Africa, and in Australia. The best known are the cobras and the mambas. Elapids have

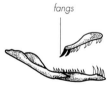

This Australian "cat snake" has poisonous fangs far back in the upper jaw. Rear-fanged snakes are rarely dangerous to humans.

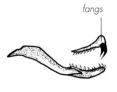

The taipan of Australia, which can be up to 13 feet (4 meters) long, is among the most dangerous poisonous snakes in the world. Elapids have fixed poisonous teeth at the front of their upper jaws.

they are so distracted that they often don't flee when they detect sounds.

Of the approximately 2,500 snake species that live on Earth, about 2,100

short, fixed poisonous fangs in the front of their upper jaws. Their venom usually causes paralysis of the nerves. In some species the poison is especially powerful.

The bite of the Indian king cobra or the Australian taipan can kill a person within fifteen minutes.

American rattlesnakes and lance-head vipers belong to the viper group. So do the common European viper, the European asp viper, the sand viper, the Orsini's viper, and the Spanish Lataste's viper. Vipers have very long poisonous fangs, which they keep tucked back when their mouths are closed. When their mouths are open, they can point their fangs forward as they suddenly open their mouths. This makes vipers very effective killers. The saw-scaled viper, for example—a viper found in Africa and Asia that is only about 20 inches (50 centimeters) long—has killed more humans than any other species of snake.

Above: *The Russell's viper, which can be up to 5 feet (1.5 meters) long, is one of the most feared poisonous snakes in Asia.*
Below: *The rattlesnake's name comes from the rattle at the end of its tail, which is shaken as a warning when the snake is threatened or disturbed.*

Below: *Rattlesnakes have long poisonous fangs that are held back when their mouths are closed. The fangs are pointed forward when they bite.*

fang

FROGS, TOADS, AND SALAMANDERS

◆ ◆ ◆ ◆ ◆ ◆ ◆ ◆ ◆ ◆ ◆

The poison of some amphibians is more toxic than the venom of even the most dangerous snakes.

Plinius Secundus was a well-known natural scientist 2,000 years ago. In his book *Historia Naturalis* he wrote: "Among all the poisonous animals, the salamander is the guiltiest. Other animals injure only a few and don't kill many at the same time. The salamander, however, is able to wipe out whole peoples." How Plinius was able to come up with this total nonsense is a puzzle, since in his time salamanders were no more dangerous than they are today! But he was right about one thing: some salamanders are poisonous.

If a predatory animal takes a salamander in its mouth in order to eat it, the predator will most likely spit it out in an instant. It may even appear to be in great pain. Most often, the predator will not die, but the painful experience is an important lesson: Leave salamanders alone.

Although bright colors are often warning signals in nature, many amphibians prove that poisonous animals don't all

The fire salamander warns of its poisonous skin with its yellow-and-black coloring.

have warning colors. Most toads and frogs, in fact, have dull camouflage colors—brownish or green—that match their surroundings. Tree frogs and a few other species can even change the color of their skin, making themselves even more "invisible." And yet they are poisonous. The poison of the homely European common toad, for example, is just about as strong as that of the fire salamander.

tiny germs. The skin of amphibians is, after all, permanently moist and therefore especially at risk—funguses and bacteria thrive especially well on a moist surface. Such funguses and bacteria are especially numerous in the warm, moist climate

Common toads are not brightly colored but can be just as poisonous as salamanders.

Recent research has proven that frogs, toads, and salamanders produce poison in their skin primarily to protect themselves from bacteria, funguses, and other

of the tropical rainforests. For amphibians that live here, a protective poison skin is particularly important. For this reason, many rainforest frogs produce extremely strong skin poison. And these frogs usually have the greatest variety of bright warning colors.

The Indians in the rainforests of South and Central America have known about frog poison for a long time. They use the poison on the tips of their arrows. That is why many poisonous rainforest frogs brought along on the hunt in small baskets. If a poison-tipped arrow is needed to kill prey that has been spotted, the Indians simply run an arrow tip over the skin of one of the frogs. The tiniest bit of

The beautiful, colorful, and very poisonous strawberry poison-dart frog of Central America is only about .75 inches (2 centimeters) long.

This colorful poison-dart frog of Costa Rica is about 1 inch (3 centimeters) long.

are also known as "poison-arrow" or "poison-dart" frogs. To get the poison, hunters collect the frogs, kill them, and place them on thin wooden spears. Then they hold the spears over a fire. The poison, which then comes out of the skin as a whitish liquid, is collected in small containers. The most poisonous of these frogs are kept alive by the Indians and poison that ends up on the arrow tip is enough to kill most animals within minutes. If, for example, a monkey high in a tree is struck by a poisoned arrow, it becomes instantly paralyzed. Once paralyzed, the monkey can no longer hold on, and falls from the tree. By the time it hits the ground, the poison will most likely have already killed it.

Opposite page: *South and Central American Indians of the rainforest make the tips of their blow darts poisonous by using the oil from the skin of various species of frogs.*

Poison-dart frogs from the rainforests of South and Central America come in a wide variety of bright colors. Below is a small selection from over 50 known species.

The green and black poison-dart frog (top left), the dyeing poison-arrow frog (top right), the rare blue poison-arrow frog (bottom left), and Lehmann's poison-arrow frog (bottom right).

The most poisonous frog known to science was discovered in Colombia, in South America. This frog is called *Phyllobates terribilis;* that means "terrible poison-arrow frog" (photo on title page). The poison from just one of these little animals is powerful enough to kill as many as 20 adult humans!

CNIDARIANS, SEA CUCUMBERS, AND SEA STARS

❖ ❖ ❖ ❖ ❖ ❖ ❖ ❖ ❖

They look like beautiful flowers, like living stars, or like delicate glass objects, but a few of these mysterious creatures are among the most dangerous poisonous animals on Earth.

People who come in contact with a sea wasp while swimming risk dying within a few minutes. This unusual creature is considered by many scientists to be the most poisonous creature on Earth. A sea wasp is a type of jellyfish. It is found on the northern Australian coast, near the Philippines, and in the Indian Ocean.

Stinging Cell

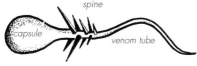

Left: *Sea anemonies look like ocean flowers but are actually poisonous animals. Oddly, the stinging cells in their tentacles, which are fatal to small living creatures, have no effect on these clown fish.*
Above: *Numerous tiny stinging cells are found in the skin of cnidarians. When the trigger is touched, the tip of the poison tube shoots into the skin of the victim like a harpoon.*

Fortunately, it appears on the beach only at certain times of year.

Jellyfish (also called medusas) are animals that swim around freely in the ocean. They consist of a transparent, glass-like body wall sometimes called a bell. Long, tentacles, there are thousands of tiny stinging cells that are filled with venom. If a prey animal comes into contact with these cells, it is paralyzed or killed. Then the victim is pulled into the body, and slowly digested inside the sac-like stomach.

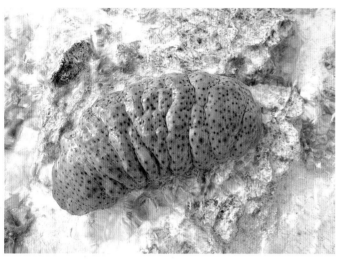

grabbing threads, the tentacles, hang from their undersides. The bell usually measures 2 to 8 inches (2 to 40 centimeters), but in the biggest species it is over 6 feet (2 meters). On the threads of the

Sea cucumbers (top left) crawl slowly around the ocean floor and feed on tiny animals and plant material. Some species can defend themselves against enemies by discharging poison.
Sea stars, of which there are many different shapes (top right, bottom), kill mussels, snails, and small crabs with a poisonous digestive liquid.

There are many different species of jellyfish, and they are found in every ocean. Only a very few of these species can be life-threatening.

Numerous poisonous stinging cells each contain a tiny venom capsule called

Above: *Hundreds of tiny coral polyps with poisonous stinging cells live in hard, often beautiful coral colonies. Right: The lamp jellyfish, which is a common resident of the Mediterranean and the warm parts of the Atlantic, has a bell that is only 3 inches (8 centimeters) long.*

a nematocyst. Inside this capsule is a thin, rolled-up venom tube. On the surface is a bristle. If an animal touches this bristle, it penetrates the skin like a harpoon and leaves its poison inside.

There are about 11,000 different species of cnidarians. Almost all are ocean dwellers. Cnidarians consist of jellyfish, hydras, sea anemones, and corals. Most kill their prey with stinging cells.

Various other ocean creatures are poisonous, too. Echinoderms, of which there are about 6,000 species, are another example. They include sea urchins, sea stars, sea cucumbers, sand dollars, and crinoids. Many sea stars secrete a poisonous slime that they use to kill their prey, which may be mussels, snails, or small crabs. The poison of sea urchins and sea cucumbers serves mainly as a defense against enemies. The sea urchin poses the greatest threat to humans. If someone steps on a sea urchin in shallow water, the spines, which are as hard as glass, penetrate deep into the skin. Inside the skin, they break open and are very difficult to remove. This causes great pain that can often last for many days.

SHELLFISH, SLUGS, AND CEPHALOPODS

◆ ◆ ◆ ◆ ◆ ◆ ◆ ◆ ◆ ◆ ◆ ◆ ◆ ◆ ◆ ◆

*Slugs aren't found only in gardens.
They are also in the ocean. Some of them
are beautiful—and quite poisonous!*

In seafood restaurants, shellfish are usually taken off the menu in the months of May through August. During these "months without an 'r,'" many shellfish ingest certain poisonous materials. These

While these poisons are in their systems, the otherwise edible hard-shelled creatures become poisonous. Shellfish take in various poisons, so the threat of poisonings isn't always the same. In most cases,

The small, beautifully colored sea slugs called nudibranchs—of which there is a wide variety of species—make themselves poisonous by eating cnidarians and storing the poison capsules in the gill-like structures on their backs.

poisons are stored in their bodies for a certain period of time, with their food.

people become sick about ten hours after eating poisonous shellfish. The most common symptoms include vomiting, stomachaches, and diarrhea. Certain other poisons, however, take effect more quickly and can cause temporary paralysis or blindness. In rare cases, these poisons can even cause death.

Most cephalopods are harmless, but a few species can severely poison humans. The cuttlefish pictured here is a member of the Sepia genus.

Nudibranchs are sea slugs. Many species are very beautifully colored. On their backs, they have gill-like structures called cerata that look like tiny trees or butterfly wings. These sea slugs often live in coral reefs, which are also brightly colored. Many nudibranchs are nonpoisonous, but they have developed a special poison trick: they feed on cnidarians. Apparently, nudibranch bodies have chemicals that prevent the otherwise dangerous cnidarians from injecting their poison. Nudibranchs can swallow cnidarians along with their poison capsules. The capsules, however, are not digested. Instead, they travel through the intestines and into the cerata, where they are used as a poisonous form of protection. Nudibranchs actually use the poisonous weapons of other animals as their own defense against enemies.

Cephalopods is the group of mollusks that includes cuttlefish, squids, octopods, and nautili. Almost all are harmless. But there are exceptions. If, for example, a person is bitten by a blue-ring octopus on the Australian coast, at first he or she won't feel a thing. But, hours later, the poison will cause serious trouble: lost feeling in the arms and legs, and blindness for hours or days. A human can even suffocate from paralysis of the lungs.

POISONOUS FISH

◆ ◆ ◆ ◆ ◆ ◆ ◆ ◆ ◆ ◆ ◆ ◆ ◆ ◆

Sharks certainly spread fear and dread, but on some tropical coasts there are little fish with poisonous spines that are much more dangerous than any great white!

On many tropical coasts, it is best not to wade around barefoot. In these waters live the world's most dangerous poisonous fish. They lie motionless, buried in sand on the ocean floor. Because they are as common-looking as stones, they are called stonefish. These creatures have spines on their backs that are connected to poison glands. If a person steps on one of these fish with bare feet, he or she

When a moray eel bites, its poisonous saliva gets into the wound.

can be severely poisoned. More than half the victims die. For the others, it is weeks before they are healthy again.

Morays are members of the eel family that live mainly in tropical and subtropical areas. They have long, snake-like bodies. They are similar to snakes in another way: many are poisonous. During the day, morays remain mostly hidden. At night, they come out of their burrows to hunt for fish and other sea creatures. Morays have poison glands in their mouths, and if they bite prey with their pointy teeth, the poison goes deep into the wounds. Some species of morays are also life-threatening to humans.

Because the flesh of morays is not poisonous and tastes delicious, they are hunted for food in some parts of the world. The ancient Romans raised morays in special bowls (these were the first aquariums in Europe).

The showy lionfish is among the most poisonous of all fishes. Lionfish belong to a very rare group of fish that use their poison as more than a defense. When these fish hunt, they approach a prey animal slowly, with their back spines pointed forward. Then they try to pierce the prey's body with a sudden jab. In this way, the lionfish is an expert swordsman.

Above: *The stonefish lies as inconspicuous as a rock on the floor of tropical seas. Anyone who steps on one with bare feet will suffer serious poisoning.*
Left: *The lionfish has a powerful poison in its spines, but it is so easy to see that creatures rarely come upon it by accident.*

SCORPIONS AND CENTIPEDES

These creepy crawlies are among the world's most feared poisonous animals—and for good reason.

Worldwide there are 1,500 to 2,000 species of scorpions. Most live in tropical and subtropical regions. About two dozen species are not only dangerous but also very common. Cracks and crevices of human homes are among their favorite places to live, mostly because in warm countries there are often a large number of cockroaches and other "house insects" on which to feed.

Until about 50 years ago, scorpions caused roughly twice as many accidents as snakes, spiders, and insects combined. With better home construction, better cleanliness in the home, regular wearing of shoes, and good medicines (antivenins), this danger has been greatly reduced. Still, about 150,000 people a year are stung by dangerous scorpions.

The scorpion's large poison stinger sits at the end of a long, moveable tail. While hunting, scorpions grasp their prey with their pincers. If the prey is large or fights back, the scorpion will flick its tail forward, over its back, and deliver a deadly dose of poison.

Scorpions are solitary animals that like to hunt at night. It is rare to see a scorpion in the middle of the day. Scorpions even prefer to avoid each other. Males

Many scorpions, such as most in southern Europe, are completely harmless. Here a mother scorpion carries her little white young.

and females only come together to mate, which is a dangerous business for the male: it's not unusual for a female to grasp the male during mating, kill him, and then eat him. Fortunately, she cares for her young a bit more lovingly. A scorpion mother carries her young, which are snow white at first, on her back, where they are well protected.

Worm-like creatures called centipedes are another kind of predator that uses poisonous weapons. Small centipedes found in gardens are quite harmless, but larger ones can be quite dangerous. In southern Europe, there is a species that is about 7 inches (17 centimeters) long and has a bite that causes severe pain. Centipedes have a pair of venom glands

Emperor scorpions are large but relatively harmless. Their venom gland, with its sizable stinger, sits at the end of the scorpion's long tail.

Among the most feared species of scorpion is the light-colored fat-tailed scorpion of Africa. Its sting can be extremely dangerous.

Centipedes can kill smaller prey animals with poisonous claws.

on the underside of their head that end in two poisonous claws. With some giant tropical species, a bite from these claws leads to severe and long-lasting poisoning. In a few cases, young children who were bitten have even died.

 SPIDERS

◆ ◆ ◆ ◆ ◆

*Many people are afraid of them, yet they
are almost all quite harmless. In fact,
we probably could not live without them.*

Many people have a terrible fear of spiders. But these fears are often overblown—even though almost all spiders are venomous.

Today, more than 37,000 different species of spider are known. Almost all

spiders have two venom glands at the front of their heads and two downward-pointing poisonous fangs. They grasp prey animals with these fangs and inject their poison which causes paralysis and usually death within a few seconds. The fangs are often large, but in most species they are too weak to pierce human skin.

One of the world's most poisonous spiders is found in Europe. It is the yellow-sac spider. This spider spends the day hidden in its web, and it is rare to see one. Its bite is very painful, and its poison is strong. The pain only wears off after several hours, and the spot that was bitten may itch all day.

The tarantula, a wolf spider found in southern Italy, is famous for its poisonous sting. People once believed that anyone bitten by this spider had to dance

———————

A yellow crab spider with a captured butterfly. Almost all spiders have poisonous fangs for catching prey, but very few species are dangerous to humans.

Above: *The male tube spider has a bright "warning" coloration that makes it appear to be dangerous. In fact, it is quite harmless.*
Right: *A bite from a yellow-sac spider can hurt for hours.*

around wildly, otherwise they would go mad. Eventually, a fast, whirling dance developed in Naples, which is now called the "tarantella," named after this spider. In fact, the bite of a tarantula is no more dangerous than a bee sting.

It would be much more serious if a black widow were to bite. It wouldn't hurt much at first, but after a few hours terrible symptoms would begin: abdominal pain, shortness of breath, nausea, headache, and trembling. Usually these symptoms will last two to three days. In very rare cases, death can even occur.

One of the most poisonous spiders in the world is the huntsman spider of the genus *Phoneutria*. It lives in South America and is about 2 inches (5 centimeters) long. This spider is unusually aggressive. It will leap without hesitation—even at a human, if he or she comes too close. Healthy adults can usually recover from a huntsman's bite after a few days, but for children and weak or sickly people, the poison from this tiny creature is often deadly.

With few exceptions, spiders are relatively harmless to humans. In fact, most

Above: *Hairy tropical tarantulas are large and "creepy looking," but are hardly dangerous.*

Below: *A black widow—shown here with her egg sac—is quite small and inconspicuous. Its bite, however, can be fatal.*

The vast majority of spiders are not especially colorful. Among the flashiest species is this harmless, metallic-colored jumping spider from Australia.

The Australian huntsman spider has giant and scary looking poisonous fangs, but it is harmless.

downward-pointing fangs of tarantula   fangs of more common spiders

Below: *Tropical spiny-bodied spiders are bizarre, vividly colored, but harmless. They are actually relatives of the common garden spider.*

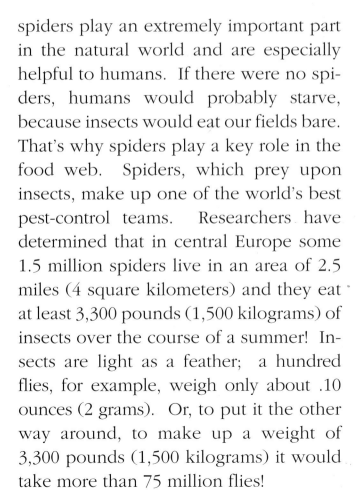

spiders play an extremely important part in the natural world and are especially helpful to humans. If there were no spiders, humans would probably starve, because insects would eat our fields bare. That's why spiders play a key role in the food web. Spiders, which prey upon insects, make up one of the world's best pest-control teams. Researchers have determined that in central Europe some 1.5 million spiders live in an area of 2.5 miles (4 square kilometers) and they eat at least 3,300 pounds (1,500 kilograms) of insects over the course of a summer! Insects are light as a feather; a hundred flies, for example, weigh only about .10 ounces (2 grams). Or, to put it the other way around, to make up a weight of 3,300 pounds (1,500 kilograms) it would take more than 75 million flies!

*I*NSECTS

◆ ◆ ◆ ◆ ◆

As a group, their battery of chemical defenses is great.

Some 750,000 to 1 million species of insects are known by science today. It is estimated that thousands more are yet undiscovered. Their lifestyles are varied. Some drink plant juices. Some are

A few tropical grasshoppers warn their enemies with flashy displays of bright colors. When in danger, they can spray a foul-smelling liquid as a means of defense.

predators. Most have specialized piercing and sucking mouthparts for feeding. To protect themselves, many produce poison.

An insect's poison is almost always used as a defensive weapon. Many species have poison strong enough to kill enemy insects—through touch contact alone. If the poison gets onto the surface of another insect's body, it dissolves the hard exoskeleton that protects the outside of an insect's body. Once the exoskeleton of an insect is gone, the insect will die.

It is always advisable to be especially careful around brightly colored insects. This is even true for caterpillars. The hairs of certain caterpillars can cause severe inflammations if they get into human eyes. In the tropics and in North America, some caterpillars have hairs so poisonous that, if they come in contact with human skin, they can cause severe burning pain.

Like many animals, many plants use poison as their main protection. Some insects use the poison in plants for their own protection. Certain butterfly species will lay their eggs only on poisonous

Some of nature's most brightly colored insects include the European red-and-black striped shield bug (above) and the assassin bug (center).
Right: *The especially colorful African shield bug.*

plants. The poison doesn't hurt the little caterpillars that hatch from the eggs. On the contrary! As they grow, the tiny caterpillars store the plants' toxic material in their bodies and thus become poisonous themselves. They even remain poisonous through the pupal stage. In South Africa, some butterfly pupae are so poisonous that the native peoples use them to poison their darts when hunting—just as certain species of poisonous frogs are used in hunting by rainforest Indians in South America.

Many "harmless" insects, including beetles, earwigs, and some grasshoppers,

Top left: *Caterpillars like this European stretch-foot caterpillar often have poisonous hairs and signal this fact with warning colors.*
This Brazilian butterfly caterpillar also warns with bright colors (top right).
The African disgusting butterfly (center) and the common ladybug (right) are also both colorful and poisonous.

poison sac

stinger shield
poison canal
stinger barb — stinger barb

sawtoothed barb tip

The hornet (top left) is greatly feared despite its size. It is much less aggressive and no more poisonous than many common wasps (top right).

Diagram: The honeybee can only sting once: the stinger stays in the wound when the bee stings, and the bee dies afterwards. The common honeybee (below left) is peaceable if it is not disturbed. The South American killer bee (below right), unlike most bees, is very aggressive.

have the same poisonous body secretions that more dangerous insects are famous for. Of course, bees, wasps, bumblebees, and ants have all proven their dangers to humans. They each have a weapon in the rear part of their bodies that works as a movable stinger. Bites and stings from these animals are probably the most common poisonous attacks that humans all over the world face each day. Most of the time these attacks are little more than

nuisances and do not cause serious damage. Unless someone is allergic, the average healthy person can survive several hundred bee stings and probably just as many from wasps and hornets.

Ants are actually closely related to wasps. Ancient ant species also had a poisonous stinger, just as wasps do today. Some species could give extremely painful stings with this stinger. But among the majority of ants, the poisonous stinger has disappeared. Nonetheless, they are not entirely without weapons. Some species have huge jaws (mandibles) with which they can deliver a powerful bite—even one that can seriously hurt a human! Many can also spray toxic chemicals from their hindquarters into a bite wound, causing a serious burning pain.

Some ants, such as this Australian bulldog ant, have a poisonous stinger.

Many ants, like this African army ant, have large jaws called mandibles for weapons. They often spray toxic chemicals into the bite.

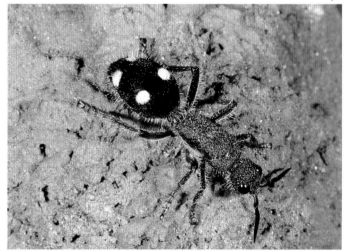

The velvet ant, a kind of wasp, has a relatively large poisonous stinger. The female has no wings and looks very much like an ant.

THE DUCKBILL PLATYPUS

◆ ◆ ◆ ◆ ◆ ◆ ◆ ◆ ◆ ◆ ◆ ◆ ◆ ◆ ◆ ◆ ◆ ◆

It looks like a beaver. It swims like a beaver.
But it has a duck's beak. It lives in the
water, but it lays eggs. It's also poisonous.

The Australian duckbill platypus is surely the oddest mammal in the world. Its body, with its thick, soft coat looks like the body of a mammal—somewhat like a beaver. But the animal has a wide, flat, horny beak like a duck. At a few spots on its body, it has scales like a lizard! And it

The male duckbill platypus is one of the few mammals in the world that has a poisonous weapon.

lays eggs. Even stranger, the female has no milk teats as do all other mammals. But she does have milk glands on her belly and can excrete milk for the young to drink.

The platypus is one of the few poisonous mammals in the world.

The male duckbill platypus has a hollow spine on the ankle joint of its hind legs that is connected to a venom gland. A zookeeper in Melbourne, Australia, who was stung by one of these spines fell to the floor in pain. His whole arm became severely swollen, and the man lay weakened for a month. Only the male platypus has this poisonous spine.

Platypuses dig holes on the embankments of rivers and lakes. They spend almost their entire lives in these burrows and in the water. They are only very rarely seen on land. They feel for their food with their sensitive beaks on the bottom of the river or lake: worms, snails, mussels, insect larvae, and crabs.

$\mathcal{T}$HE STRONG AND THE SHOWY

◆ ◆ ◆ ◆ ◆ ◆ ◆ ◆ ◆ ◆

Poisonous animals often alert their enemies with bright warning colors. But there are many completely harmless animals that have learned to benefit from this trick.

Bumblebees (above) *are feared because they have a poisonous stinger at their disposal in case of emergency. Various harmless insects imitate the well-defended bumblebee, including the bumblebee fly* (above right) *and the bumblebee hawkmoth, a butterfly* (right).

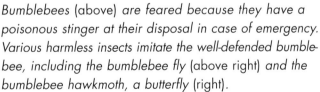

In a flower meadow, you may spot an insect that looks like a bumblebee. It flies from flower to flower like a bumblebee, and hums like a bumblebee. But if

The wasp, which is equipped with a poisonous stinger, has a particularly large number of defenseless imitators.

Here is a line-up of "wasp-mimics": a hover fly (above), a beetle called the long-horned wasp beetle (below), and the wasp spider (bottom).

you looked at it under a microscope, you would find that it is just a harmless fly. With its "disguise," it imitates a dangerous bumblebee to perfection. The bumblebee fly's mimicry is perfect—and as a result, it also has a few enemies.

The Greek word *mimikry* means "imitation." What the bumblebee fly does—and many other animals in the natural world—is called "Batesian mimicry." This type of imitation was discovered by an English natural scientist named Henry Walter Bates. Bates crossed the rainforests of the Amazon around 1850. An excellent observer, he discovered various beetles, butterflies, flies, and other harmless insects that looked like dangerous bees, wasps, or ants. He suspected that this could not be an accident. He then discovered that it was actually a very special survival trick. By posing as dangerous or poisonous animals, the harmless imitators could protect themselves against enemies. And the more precise the disguise, the greater the insect's success.

Different caterpillars imitate dangerous snakes with "eye" or scale markings designed to look like poisonous snakes. Some even have skin structures that look like the split tongue of a snake! Some caterpillars in Southeast Asia do this as a group performance. When searching for a new plant to feed on, they crowd together in the thousands and move forward together so nimbly that they look like a 3-foot (1-meter) crawling snake.

Although these bluffers belong to an entirely different butterfly family, they look exactly like the poisonous, narrow-winged Heliconiidae. They are so close in appearance that people often can't tell the difference without a magnifying lens.

There are also imitators among other animals. In North America, there are coral snakes that have a beautiful red-black-yellow ring pattern. These are warning colors that announce the snake's dangerous nature. There are, however, also "false coral snakes." These too are vividly patterned with red, black, and yellow rings—but they are completely harmless. The viperine snake is found in southern

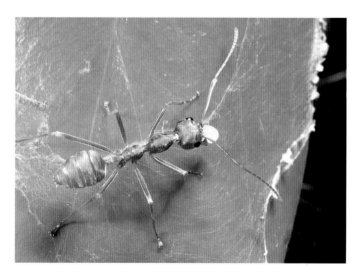

In South and Central America, there is a whole series of poisonous butterfly species with narrow, red-black-and-yellow wings, members of the Heliconiidae family. These poisonous butterflies have in turn a whole group of harmless imitators.

Above left: *The well-defended ant also has its imitators. Here you can see a weaver ant, which can bite and spray poison into the bite.*
Above: *This is a completely harmless ant spider.*

Europe northward to southwestern Switzerland. These snakes got their name because they have a dark spotted or zigzag marking on their light-colored backs, just like a poisonous viper. If these harmless water snakes feel directly threatened, they can perform an astounding act of animal mimicry: they imitate the attack posture of the viper, hiss, and puff themselves up. As they do this, their bodies and heads become much bigger. In the process, they look so precisely like a dangerous viper that even a snake expert has to look twice before picking one up!

In North America various species of coral snakes are as colorful as they are poisonous.

North America is also home to some very similarly colored but nonetheless completely nonpoisonous "false coral snakes."

PREVENTION IS ALWAYS BEST

❖ ❖ ❖ ❖ ❖ ❖ ❖ ❖ ❖ ❖ ❖ ❖

A famous proverb says that prevention is better than a cure. With the proper knowledge, respect, and caution, you can avoid accidents with poisonous animals.

As this book shows, there are plenty of poisonous animals on our beautiful Earth. But the vast majority of them are harmless to humans.

Wasps and bees probably deserve the greatest respect of all poisonous animals. Even though they are far from the most poisonous animals, they still cause the most serious accidents. An average, healthy person can survive a few hundred wasp or bee stings, but there are people that are oversensitive (allergic) to these animals. These people must be treated by a doctor immediately after being stung. If they do not get immediate treatment, the sting could be life-threatening.

The danger of being bitten by a snake is much less than being stung by a wasp or bee. Still, snakes are very common in forested areas, as well as in grassy fields. It is best not to walk or hike barefoot in any such place. You should go barefoot only on open, well-maintained ground. Most accidents occur because of careless barefoot walking. Also pay attention when collecting berries, mushrooms, and wood: Keep an eye on where you're grabbing. Be careful if you sit on a pile of rocks or wood, since these are favorite hiding places for snakes! Even with all this caution, however, a poisonous snake bite can occur. That means acting as quickly but as calmly as possible.

Most people are bitten in the leg or the hand. In these cases, it is relatively easy to prevent the poison from spreading quickly throughout the body. Limbs are often tied off about a hand's width above the bite. An elastic bandage, suspenders, or a rubber tube is often used for this. A rolled-up handkerchief, under which a pencil or something similar is pushed so that turning the pencil will tighten it, will also do. Never use a cord or string to tie the wound off! If you are ever faced with this emergency, remember: Only tighten enough for the limb to become red or bluish-red. Don't tie it so tight that blood circulation is cut off completely. If the tie is too tight, the limb will turn white and can go numb. About

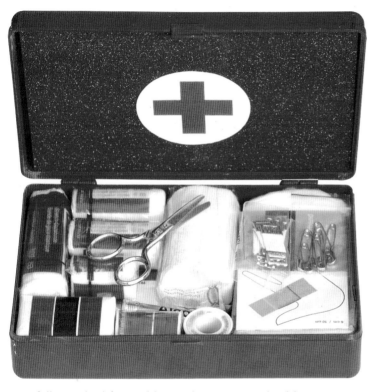

A fully stocked first-aid kit is always a good addition to any trip.

every half-hour, the tie should be briefly loosened. If you're the least bit uncertain, it is better to have nothing at all than a bad or incorrect tie! Many years ago, cutting out, sucking out, or burning out the wound was recommended. Today, this should absolutely be avoided. It usually does more harm than good!

The most important thing: Keep the victim as still as possible and find a doctor right away.

Extra caution is needed for travels to foreign countries, especially to the tropics. Buy a good travel guide in advance; it will describe and maybe even picture possible poisonous animals you may encounter. Where there are poisonous snakes and scorpions, it is always wise to wear good shoes. Never reach into any crevices or holes, and arm yourself at night—even in a hotel or cabin!—with a good flashlight. And watch out when swimming in lakes or seas. Observe warning signs, look out for jellyfish, and always go into the water with beach shoes on, even if the other swimmers haven't. Stonefish, stingrays, and a whole host of potential poisoners can be hidden in the sand.

A final word on the subject of poison: Five hundred years ago a doctor and natural scientist named Paracelsus discovered the significance of poisonous materials. He said, "All things are poison and nothing is without poison. Only the dose makes a thing not a poison."

Doctors thousands of years ago in ancient Greece were already making certain medicines out of poisons. They knew how to use poison and skin from snakes in the production of special kinds of medications.

They also worshipped Asclepius, the Greek god of medicine, who took the form of a snake. The Romans also worshipped this god. Even today the symbol for the medical profession is the holy snake, which is wrapped around an Asclepian staff. You certainly know this symbol: It is shown in every pharmacy sign.

As the discoveries and practical uses of Greeks and Romans show us, poison is not really all bad. As the doctor Paracelsus said, everything is poisonous in some form—some things are simply more poisonous than others.

The poisons and weapons we find in nature all have very specific uses. Nearly all of them allow an animal to survive in some way. And an animal that survives is considered to be a success. That is why even the most poisonous or dangerous animals have a special place in nature and deserve our respect.

The African spitting cobra can deliver a dangerous bite with its poison-filled fangs. It can also spit poison up to 10 feet (3 meters) away! If this poison gets into an enemy's eyes it can cause temporary blindness.

FURTHER READING

Allen, Missy and Peissel, Michel. *Dangerous Insects* (Encyclopedia of Danger). New York: Chelsea House, 1993.

Burns, Diane L. *Snakes, Salamanders, and Lizards.* Minocqua, WI: NorthWord Press, 1995.

Grace, Eric S. and Lawrence, R.D. *Snakes* (Sierra Club Wildlife Library). San Francisco: Sierra Club Books, 1994.

Hillyard, Paul. *Spiders and Scorpions: A Look Inside.* New York: Reader's Digest 1995.

Ling, Mary. *The Snake Book.* New York: Dorling Kindersley, 1997.

Mound, Laurence. *Insect* (Eyewitness Books). New York: Random House, 1990.

Parker, Steve. *Frogs and Toads.* San Francisco: Sierra Club Books, 1994.

Taylor, Barbara. *Nature Watch: Snakes.* Dayton, OH: Lorenz Books, 1998.

Tibbitts, Christiane Kump. *Seashells, Crabs, and Sea Stars.* Minocqua, WI: NorthWord Press, 1996.

INDEX

Page numbers in bold indicate pictures.